BLOCKCHAIN
FAST AND SIMPLE:
WHAT IT IS,
HOW IT WORKS,
WHY IT MATTERS

by Piero Martini

Disclaimer

This disclaimer governs the use of this book and its content.

The information provided within this book is for general informational purposes only.

It is not advice, and should not be treated as such.

References to publicly available information, including trademarks, are without any prior consent by the owners. They are for illustrative purposes only.

Trademarks belong to the respective owners, who are not affiliated with this book.

While the author attempts to keep the information up-to-date and correct, there is no assurance or warranty, express or implied, about the completeness, accuracy, reliability, suitability or availability with respect to the information, products or services contained in this book for any purpose. Any use of this information is at your own risk.

Cover Illustration Copyright © 2017 Piero Martini

Table of Contents

Preface

'Once a new technology rolls over you, if you're not part of the steamroller, you're part of the road.'
Stewart Brand

I decided to write this book because I kept getting lots of questions from friends, relatives, and colleagues about this new technology.

I then pretty quickly realized that there was a reason for all these queries: a lot of the literature currently available was written by techies for techies.

It was (and still is) difficult for people to navigate in the vast amount of information out there in order to find simple answers to basic questions around the essence of Blockchain technology.

The primary goal here is to enable the man in the street to grasp the underlying idea of what a Blockchain is, by simplifying its terminologies and concepts while respecting the core logic. If you feel there is room for improvement or that any of the fundamentals could be better presented, please get in touch via Amazon.

To conclude: I make no claims whatsoever about this manuscript to be a top notch perfect and accurate academic piece of work. This book is just a simple alternative that may help some people get a foot in the door as regards this fantastic new piece of innovation called Blockchain.

Chapter One: Introduction

2005: Hurricane Katrina hit the Gulf Coast of the United States causing huge damage to the entire region. One of the worst discoveries in the aftermath: Years of public archives such as birth certificates and medical records were destroyed and lost forever.

2016: Wiring 50 US dollars from New York to London takes up to five days, costs more than 30 US dollars in transactions fees, and conversion to pounds sterling (so that the US dollars can be spent locally) comes at a charge.

What do these two apparently unrelated facts have in common? Their course of action is likely to be dramatically different in the future thanks to a new disruptive technology called Blockchain!

Welcome to a new paradigm where recorded data is immune to loss, physical corruption, altering, tampering, fraud, or political control; where money can be transferred at low cost, instantly, and more securely than ever before; and where information is open to everyone but controlled by no one!

You don't have to be a digital native or computer specialist to be intrigued by the potential of what experts envision as 'the best invention since the arrival of the Internet'.

Jump on board now while we're still at the beginning of the Blockchain revolution!

Chapter Two: Blockchain History

How it all began: the era of digital currencies

To understand what a Blockchain is, we need to step back into recent history and become familiar with the concept of 'digital currency'.

What is digital currency?

This is Wikipedia: 'Digital currency or digital money is an Internet-based medium of exchange distinct from physical (such as banknotes and coins) that exhibits properties similar to physical currencies, but allows for instantaneous transactions and borderless transfer-of-ownership.'

This is how I explain it: A digital currency is money created and stored electronically that you can use on the Internet!

No need for printing paper (i.e. banknotes) with lots of ink and fancy designs, no minting of coins, no pegging to gold or silver, no central bank involvement.

It's digital: you have it, own it, save it, administer it from any laptop or mobile phone, and spend it online wherever you like, whenever you like, in real time.

If we stop for a second and observe the way we operate online, we notice that we can execute 'almost' any transaction between two parties without the need for intermediaries. Take the example of

Alice and Bob, where Alice and Bob are two fictional names frequently used as placeholders in modern scientific literature in areas such as physics or information technology.

Alice can seamlessly send an email, text a message, order a taxi, or have some pizza delivered directly to Bob's doorstep.

All these actions are direct, without the need for any sort of middleman; Alice doesn't go to a physical desk to ask an operator (and pay him for the service) to take her email and deliver it to Bob, does she?

She just fires up her computer, writes the email, inserts Bob's correct destination address, and presses 'Send': Done!

So, why did we put that 'almost' in quotes?

Back to Alice: Imagine Alice wanted to send Bob 50 US dollars directly, instantaneously, and securely so that he could treat himself to a nice bottle of wine for his birthday.
Unfortunately Alice can't really do that today without using the services of a third party such as a bank, or providers like PayPal, Western Union, etc.

What's the problem with these third parties in the game?

A first issue is that their transactions are not fast, especially if they are across borders (it takes anywhere between three and five days), and they are certainly not cheap: It's actually good business for these

intermediaries. Nor are other possibilities such as micropayments –
e.g. a fraction of 1 US dollar – feasible, most likely because as of
today they're not economically viable: costs > benefits.

But here is another key point: In order to function, these kinds of
online transactions rely on 'trust'.

Alice needs to 'trust' her bank not to take the money she deposited
and add it to its CEO's bonus instead of sending it to Bob. Bob
needs to 'trust' his bank not to forget to credit his account with the
50 US dollars when they arrive from Alice.
Then they both need to 'trust' the entire interconnected banking
system to act as a proper clearing house, thus ensuring that the
money transferred is not fake, that Alice can only send money that
she actually owns, and that the money only gets delivered to Bob's
correct account. And so on, and so on, and so on.

This is a problem: this whole trust mechanism is slow, rigid, and
expensive.

… so here's a clue: the Internet, so developed in many aspects, was
still pretty primitive when it came to executing transfers of value. It
needed to find a way to carry out these transactions in a securer and
more efficient way. Which is where the idea of digital currencies
was born!

Digital currencies started making an appearance when the Internet
was in its infancy, somewhere around the mid-1990s. A few initial

experiments were tried out, like e-gold, a gold-backed digital currency which enjoyed discreet success before being quickly binned due to malicious (hackers') attacks or regulatory interventions.

Until recently, however, there had been no significant breakthrough even though the concept of digital currencies was not now completely foreign to us: online gaming had been using them for a long time, and gift cards or airline miles could be thought of as a kind of digital currency.

Now let's dig a bit deeper into a special subcategory of digital currencies called cryptocurrencies.

Compared with simple digital currencies, cryptocurrencies have an additional specific feature that makes them unique: they are extremely secure to use online because they're based on state-of-the-art cryptography.

So why do cryptocurrencies matter?

The importance of Bitcoin

Bitcoin, the first significant example of a cryptocurrency, was born in October 2008 with the publication of 'Bitcoin: A Peer-to-Peer Electronic Cash System,' a paper written by Satoshi Nakamoto.

Note that Satoshi Nakamoto is an alias; his/her/their real identity so far remains unknown despite multiple failed attempts to track him/her/them down.

The new currency named Bitcoin was based on computer code and released in January 2009 as an open source (meaning software open to anyone to use, adopt, and modify without copyrights or legal restrictions).

Shortly thereafter, Satoshi Nakamoto mysteriously disappeared from the public scene – i.e. forums, papers, etc. – in April 2011. Even in Satoshi Nakamoto' absence, Bitcoin continued to develop and grew fast. It was not until 2013, however, that it gained popularity as more and more websites started accepting this new currency, investors started pouring money into a booming startup scene, and early adopters' communities grew in size.

Why did this relatively peculiar idea become a success, with billions of US dollars in market capitalization?

Here are some reasons why:

- It doesn't need the services of a middleman to run so no banks, agencies, or brokers involved

- It works directly between users without the need for them to 'trust' or even know each other

- It's private and allows for a high degree of anonymity

- It runs on a decentralized infrastructure, not controlled by any single central authority such as a government

- It's public so everyone can see everything

- It's extremely secure (thanks to cryptography)

- It's resistant to inflation since supply is limited

- It's cheap: one can execute transactions for the equivalent of fractions of US dollars, euros, etc.

All solid points, but Bitcoin has an additional major strength: it solves an old genetic issue of digital currencies called the 'double spending' problem.

'Double spending' essentially means spending the same money more than once.

Think of when you send a PDF document via email. The original of that PDF may be with you, but you can send a specified number of copies to all your friends. While this is fine when it comes to documents such as PDFs, it's a problem when it comes to money.

What if you were to make a perfect paper copy of a banknote in your wallet and use that copy in a grocery store?

That's exactly when you'd be 'double spending' the amount of value corresponding to your original banknote.

This (bad) behaviour is not acceptable because it creates a systemic issue: in the long run, nobody would know which banknote was valid and which was not, what was the real value represented by a banknote, etc.

In other words, we would be destroying value instead of preserving it.

Bitcoin managed to make every token of its digital currency traceable, secure, and unique: no chance of duplicating a single unit of Bitcoin. In other words, nobody can simply copy let alone 'print' more Bitcoins as some central governments do with their national currencies from time to time.

To sum up: There is no question that Bitcoin encountered huge hype and became very popular as pioneers started seeing it not only as a valid way to transfer money but also to store value.

But, but, but... there was another piece of the equation that went unnoticed by the vast majority for quite some time. A pretty fundamental one!

Bitcoin was based on a brand new technology called Blockchain.

As time went by, people started realizing that this new underlying technology could effectively be decoupled from the cryptocurrency itself. Blockchain alone could be adopted to do much more than just exchanging native digital tokens, i.e. Bitcoins.

This is where it all began and how the whole idea of Blockchain came to the attention of the general public.

Chapter Three: What Is a Blockchain

A definition

To be honest, none of the main definitions I found out there were particularly intuitive. They are understandable but it becomes difficult to grasp the real basics of a Blockchain without getting lost in the bits and bytes of tech jargon. Here are some examples:

- A Blockchain is a decentralized, public ledger that contains the details of every transaction that has ever been completed...

- A Blockchain is an ever-lengthening chain of blocks...

- A Blockchain is distributed ledger technology...

Got it? Sort of, I guess.

Here is my best attempt (for now): A Blockchain is a huge file which stores data in a logical, historical, secure, and immutable way.

And here are two parallels that helped me in the first place:

- A Blockchain is like a big book. A book represents data (e.g. text) recorded in pages, following a logical structure

- A Blockchain is like a huge Excel sheet (or database, or a long list of records, if you prefer), where all the information contained gets recorded in the same way, is validated before entering the Excel sheet, and cannot be unilaterally modified

A bit better now, perhaps, but still not there yet.

Let's take a closer look at the mechanics of a Blockchain to figure out how it works.

What does a Blockchain do?

A Blockchain is all about organizing and storing information in accordance with a predefined logic.

Exactly as in a history book which contains a track record of events, with descriptive text organized in pages and ordered by numbers, a Blockchain stores information in a chronological, indexed, and ordered way.

What kind of information?

Most prominent examples are currently related to financial transactions (e.g. money transfers), but the technology can apply more or less to anything with value attached (not necessarily only monetary value): proof of ownership, intellectual property, health records, etc.

What are the 'ingredients' of a Blockchain?

Software

It's all based on sophisticated computer code. A Blockchain is born, lives, and dies, all as software.

Cryptography (aka hard core math)

This is relevant since it guarantees privacy, identity, and authenticity. For example, cryptography ensures that the information contained in a Blockchain cannot be pieces of information.

Hardware (actually computers)

It runs on a computer (yes, it could be your personal computer), not just one computer but lots of them. A network of computers! The computers in this network, usually referred to as peer-to-peer, are all connected to each other. They are all 'peers' and so in a sense equals. This is different from today's world where most of the applications we use run on centralized architecture, like your PC connecting to a webserver to download a webpage. This is important since it tells us a Blockchain is 'distributed', precisely because it's not running in a single place, as may be the case with your email account operated out of some email servers from a provider like Google. It lives and replicates across its network, in almost real time.

The Internet

This is the glue, it's how the network above connects, interacts, replicates, and operates.

Basic components of a Blockchain

Very simply put, a Blockchain is composed of transactions and blocks. To be more correct, it's a sequence of **transactions** and **blocks**.

Transactions

This is the real foundation stone. Transactions represent operations that transfer, or change, the value of tangible or intangible assets between different parties.

In our 50 US dollars example: when Alice wants to send Bob 50 US dollars, what she's really doing is transferring value (the 50 US dollars then become Bob's property) so she is generating a transaction.

A transaction in a Blockchain is represented by converting some input information ('Send 50 US dollars from Alice to Bob') into a secure yet humanly unreadable, unique digital output by using a conversation algorithm called Hashing.

This results in a string of hexadecimal characters (letters and numbers), called Hash.

Hashing is used throughout a Blockchain because it makes it possible to conveniently, securely, and efficiently store and process lots of information.

Moreover, hashing has some interesting properties:

- Uniqueness: the same inputs will always give the same outputs

- Safety: changing any minimal part of the input, like a single digit or bit, will generate a completely different output, i.e. Hash

- Anonymity: given the output, it's not possible to 'back trace' all the way to the input, meaning there is no way to find out what the input information was

Here is what Alice's transaction input information would look like as a Hash:

Transaction: Send 50 US dollars from Alice to Bob

Transaction Hash:
0x75a28ea8993beb2fabb7b5a012546bc8e7aede...

Blocks

Blocks are where transactions are stored.

Transactions are recorded in blocks in a linear, chronological order.

In the example of the book, we can think of the blocks as the pages whereas transactions could be the individual lines of a single page. In a Blockchain, blocks play a key role since they store multiple information concerning transactions such as the history of a transaction, associated time stamps, security parameters that regulate access to the information, addresses used, and more.

Blocks are linked to each other, like a chain, because every block contains a reference to the previous block.

This reference is also calculated applying Hashing so references are also Hashes.

The first block in a Blockchain is called the genesis block and contains basis information and parameters. It does not refer to any other previous block since it is the beginning, the very genesis.

Interesting! We begin to see how a Blockchain is forming: transactions after transactions, which get stored into blocks after blocks.

Chapter Four: How Does a Blockchain Work

To properly function, a Blockchain needs three actors: **users**, **nodes**, and **miners**.

Users

Users are the participants generating the transactions. They are active in the network, exchanging values like buying or selling items, sending and receiving money, etc. They are people like Bob, Alice, you, me.

Nodes

Nodes are all the computers connected to the network that can read and write from a Blockchain. These are the backbone of a Blockchain, like the vertebral columns in our bodies. Nodes are always connected and in sync with the network and, crucially, must have a full copy of all the transactions that have ever happened.

Okay, so now let's stop and think: if they have a copy of all the transactions, and transactions are stored in blocks, it means they have a copy of the entire Blockchain.

That's right: every node always has the latest copy of the Blockchain so it always has the latest information, in near real time.

Note: You don't need a full copy of the Blockchain to be a user. But you do need one to be a node. Nowadays a user can also use smartphone apps or websites to transfer value using a Blockchain without being a full node.

Miners

Remember that transactions are stored in blocks. But who creates these blocks? Who validates these blocks and guarantees that they're legit?

That's where the miners come into the game!

A miner is nothing other than a node that is also allowed to add a block onto the Blockchain. So your computer can be a node, simply hosting data and reading/writing transactions from/to the Blockchain, or it can also be geared up to do something more.

Miners are allowed to do this by competing to solve a special mathematical problem, which is always derived from the latest state of the Blockchain.

This mechanism is called 'proof of work'. This is where high level math is built into the system.

The miners must try multiple combinations to solve these problems ('proof of work') and identify the single correct answer every time.

That's why they are really powerful, special computers (unlike the ones we usually have at home), which can process a lot of data and are intelligent enough to perform these complex calculations.

When competing against each other in the network, the first miner to solve the math problem relevant at that point in time can add the next block onto the Blockchain, like a scientist publishing his discovery.

Why do miners 'mine'?

They get compensated by winning a reward, usually tokens of a digital currency.

In the case of the Bitcoin Blockchain, for instance, miners receive Bitcoins as a compensation for their 'work'.

Tokens can then be exchanged in the cryptocurrency market for some cash, or they can be spent in any of the numerous shops accepting them.

We can now see why they're called miners: in some way, they're constantly digging (looking for solutions to complex math problems) until they find the clue (their 'gold') and add the next block so as to get compensated (the incentive to mine).

And there is just one more step: once the miner has solved a specific problem and added a block to the Blockchain, the entire network is then obliged to update its copy of the Blockchain with that new block.

Every node syncs automatically and receives the latest information. This process can take up varying amounts of time, depending on the Blockchain.

In Bitcoin, it takes around 10 minutes.

Now we begin to understand why it's called a Blockchain.

The term Blockchain is derived from the way transactions are stored in blocks and blocks are linked: transactions are constantly processed, recorded, and updated by everyone in the network.

This is very similar to how ledgers work in classic accounting terms, for example; that's also why a Blockchain is often also referred to a 'ledger of transactions' or 'ledger technology'.

Hmm, but how does it really work?

Let's go back to the basics: transactions.

Transactions are not disconnected from each other. They're not isolated 'islands', they're more like archipelagos that know their own history. Here is why: among others, a transaction typically also contains a reference to previous transactions and a reference to where the outcome of the transaction itself – the output – should go.

Within 'Send 50 US dollars from Alice to Bob', for example, there will be a reference to a previous transaction stored in a block somewhere along the chain, where it's recorded not only that Alice is the owner but also how, where from, when, she received those 50 US dollars. In the book example, this reference would be like scrolling backwards in the book to a certain page and finding a certain line stating 'Alice receives 50 US dollars from Paul, sent from this address, on Tuesday December 11, December 2010, at 11.15 AM'.

Once a transaction is requested, it's broadcast to the network: when Alice initiates 'Send 50 US dollars from Alice to Bob', this request gets sent out to all the nodes.

Why? Because every transaction needs to be validated by the entire network before being added to a block!

Remember the 'double spending' issue we mentioned before?

When Alice wants to send Bob 50 US dollars using a digital currency, she is not physically transferring a banknote. She's sending the equivalent of a digital file but, since these files are digital, how can we distinguish with certainty the original from scam copies?

Also, what if Alice didn't really have those 50 US dollars to begin with? How would Bob know whether Alice was really the owner of those 50 US dollars and whether, once sent, they were officially no longer in her possession but in his?

If we think of today's financial systems, that's what a clearing house or bank does for us and charges a high fee.

Banks constantly update their ledgers to record the fact that Alice has enough funds, that she is who she says she is (in financial services presently referred to as the Know Your Customer (KYC) procedure), and that, once the transaction is generated, Alice's account balance falls by 50 US dollars (if she had a sufficient balance in the first place otherwise it would invalidate the transaction) while Bob's is increased by the same amount.

So how, then, does a Blockchain network prevent this 'double spending' issue and other problems? It uses something called a consensus mechanism.

When a transaction is broadcast, all the other participants in the network need to check that the transaction is correct in accordance with some predefined mandatory rules. For example, that the transaction contains proper valid transfer parameters such as indicating the amount of reward (i.e. the fee) for the miner who will manage to add this transaction to a block, or that the sender's balance has sufficient resources, etc.

This is the basic idea behind the consensus mechanism, which therefore enables the list of transactions to be continually expanded, shared, and validated in real time by thousands of nodes.

Now we see where the difference with the main applications in use today is: Blockchains are not centralized, but decentralized.

A Blockchain does not need a third party to operate since everyone (well, every node) has a constantly updated copy of all the transactions that ever happened! Everyone can contribute to the validation of a transaction so it becomes very difficult to cheat. Or at least it is still theoretically possible but not economically convenient.

Note that this is unlike our existing financial systems where cheats can avoid getting caught and sometimes get away with it.

So no third party, eh? This is powerful!

Who now needs all those white-collar bankers, offices, ATMs, huge buildings, etc., performing byzantine tasks?! That whole infrastructure can be dismantled and lots of money saved to the benefit of the end users: us.

The ultimate important takeaway here is that a Blockchain is basically a 'trustless' system. You do not need to know anything about the other users, or trust them as individuals, to initiate a transaction (and have faith that the system will work).

This is possible thanks to the consensus mechanism because transactions and blocks cannot be tampered with; altering them would require coordinating a lot of separate computers (nodes, miners, etc.). Everyone in the network has a valid copy of the correct history so it becomes immensely difficult to fool everyone.

Security is key(s)!

We mentioned that a Blockchain enabled secure transactions and storage of information.

But how does it do this?

Precisely as you do when you leave your house in the morning before going somewhere: you lock the door with a key. In Blockchain, you need two keys, not one.

It's already more secure. That's where cryptography comes in handy again.

Every user in the Blockchain has two keys: keys are digital, which means that there would also be a hexadecimal sequence in the end. These keys are encrypted and anonymized, meaning they're not readable to a human eye. They look something like this:

6kb8kLf9zgWQnogidDA76MzPL6TsZZY36hWXMssSzNydYXYB 9KF

The two keys are a 'public' and a 'private' one.

The public and private keys are mathematically linked and are used to 'sign' transactions, ensuring that only the rightful person gains access to the information contained therein.

The public key is different from the private one in that it has a different utility: it's basically your only identity in the Blockchain, your 'address', and it's visible to everyone on the Blockchain. In our example, 'Send 50 US dollars from Alice to Bob' is a transaction between Alice and Bob, who are represented in the Blockchain by two public addresses, nothing other than the two public keys.

Note that, in general, transactions are not encrypted so it is possible to browse and view every transaction ever collected in a Blockchain. But what can you really view?

You can only see that one address sent another address 50 US dollars at one point in time. But it's not possible to see who those 'addresses' really are, discover their identities, the streets where they live, how much money they have. Remember some of the important features of hashing? One simply finds out what the input was, starting from the output! Oh, and don't forget, transactions are secure and immutable: nobody can access transactions to modify them, e.g. cancel 'Send 50 US dollars from Alice to Bob' and instead initiate 'Send 50 US dollars from Alice back to Paul'.

'Send 50 US dollars from Alice to Bob' was signed using Bob's public key. Let's assume that Bob has received the 50 US dollars. How will he access these funds?

He uses his private key (mathematically linked to his public key). This is very important since it allows him and only him to gain access. A private key is like your front door key: if someone gets hold of it, he can enter your house!

When Alice generates the 50 US dollars transaction what she's really stating is:

'I grant the right to have these 50 US dollars received by the person who owns the private key (i.e. Bob's private key) corresponding to this address (i.e. Bob's public address).'

Basically, the 50 US dollars are in a safe deposit glass box, but only Bob now has the key to open the safe.

Chapter Five: Types of Blockchains

You may hear about this while reading of Blockchains in the future. In these highly experimental times, people sometimes easily tend to distinguish Blockchains by associating them with their native digital currency.

For example: The Bitcoin Blockchain, where the native digital currency is Bitcoin.

First of all, however, it's important to get to know the difference between the three basic types of Blockchains today: **public**, **private**, and **sidechains**.

Let's begin here: The difference between public and private Blockchains is comparable to the difference between the Internet, which is open and available to everybody, and intranets, which belong to closed organizations where access is regulated via permissions.

Public Blockchains

They are distributed and open to anyone. Transactions are public. To enforce the consistency of the system and validate transactions, financial incentives (the mining rewards described above) and consensus mechanisms are embedded into the system. Because a public Blockchain is available to anyone, improvements are only possible with the previous consensus of the network. Importantly, public Blockchains offer great potential for reducing costs (e.g. transaction fees). If we take a look at the Bitcoin network as an example, the average fee for a Bitcoin transaction is about 5 US cents, compared to more than 36 US cents for a typical third-party transaction like a credit card. Some examples (besides Bitcoin):

Ethereum – www.ethereum.org

Provider of a decentralized platform that runs on a custom-built Blockchain. It allows developers to publish distributed applications, create markets, store registries of debts or promises, and move funds around, all without a middleman or counterparty risk.

Factom – www.factom.com

Based on a customized Blockchain platform, Factom is building a system designed to track property ownership via a notarization functionality. It focuses on records that can originate from business processes for commercial and non-profit organizations and governments.

Ripple – www.ripple.com

This is perhaps a bit of a mixed one: Ripple's distributed financial technology enables banks around the world to directly transact with each other without the need for a central counterparty or correspondent. In a nutshell: instant, certain, low-cost international payments. It's mixed because even though Ripple, as in the protocol, is open source, it can be customized to the uses of a single bank or financial institution.

Private Blockchains

Private Blockchains are set up and maintained by private organizations, which only grant access to authorized parties. Transactions are verified within the private Blockchain and can potentially be modified within that private network, thus enabling operators to correct errors. This would not be accepted in a public Blockchain.

Private Blockchains can authenticate transactions more quickly – generally within seconds – because they operate on networks that are more controlled (not to say centralized) and are made of up fewer computers. Some examples:

Eris Industries – https://erisindustries.com/

Eris Industries is an application platform which standardizes many development activities when building a Blockchain-backed application. Eris's goal is to make it simple and easy for any organization to get started using permissionable, smart-contract-capable Blockchains.

R3 – www.r3cev.com

This technology company leads a consortium of (actually really big) banks which aims to provide financial institutions with smoother back-office operations such as clearing, settlement, and trading in financial instruments on a private Blockchain.

This currently represents probably the best attempt to create a standard for banking in the financial services industry.

Chain – www.chain.com

Chain Inc. provides a platform that enables trading in private company shares (but really supports any assets in any market) with the Blockchain, mainly targeted at high-scale financial networks which need compliance.

Sidechains

Sidechains are decentralized, peer-to-peer networks that provide useful enhancements (such as security, risk, and performance) and run in parallel to a main Blockchain. As an example, they enable developers to safely develop new applications without risk.

Sidechaining may also be referred to as a mechanism that allows items such as items from one Blockchain to be securely used within a completely separate Blockchain but still moved back to the original chain if necessary. By convention, the original chain is normally referred to as the 'main chain' while any additional Blockchains that enable users to transact within them in the tokens of the main chain are referred to as 'sidechains'.

Chapter Six: Why Does Blockchain Matter

… meaning what can we do with it? This is where it gets fascinating.

The list of applications as we know it today is far from complete. Blockchain is such a young technology that future developments will open up endless possibilities.

Some people compare this breakthrough with what we've seen with the Internet: a revolution that started slowly, surrounded by skepticism, but then rapidly exploded, becoming mainstream and changing our lives forever.

Some visionaries believe this is the Internet of the future, a kind of version 3.0!

Let's look at possible application types.

Smart contracts

Smart contracts are contracts that are programmed and hosted in a Blockchain and run automatically. When a certain programmed condition is triggered, the smart contract executes the terms of the agreement.

It can be seen as a traditional contract in today's terms but without the need for a lawyer to draw up complex legal terms, a notary to ratify signatures, or an escrow party to deposit a copy of the agreement: essentially, it's just software code.

Here is the classic example of a smart contract: an insurance policy for farmers. It could work like this: depending on the weather, the policy pays out based on the quantity of rainfall in a given month.

Imagine if you could safely do business with someone you don't know because the terms of the agreement were spelled out in a 'smart contract'. There could be Blockchain versions of Airbnb or eBay: no company would need to sit in the middle of a transaction to collect fees from an intermediary to process a transaction or gain access to personal data about our habits.

Fantasy? Take a look at this example: https://openbazaar.org/

Mobile peer-to-peer payment

Peer-to-peer payments are informal payments made from one person to another. Allowing them to be done via a mobile app diminishes the need for cash and checks. Blockchain acts as an enabler.

Here is an example: https://www.goabra.com/

Users need only to download the app, fund their online wallet, and send money completely free to other users by entering their phone number. In seconds! No costs! No need for a third party!

Supply chain management

This is about tracking the movement of goods in a secure (no fraud), reliable, unique, ubiquitous way: Blockchain provides an ideal platform on which a highly secure supply chain management system can be built.

Here is an example: http://chronicled.com/

Chronicled is a startup that develops solutions for authentication and tracking of brand goods: it aims at eliminating fakes forever and already enables you to 'verify a sneaker's authenticity with the tap of a mobile phone, leveraging on Blockchain'.

Here is another example: www.provenance.org

From their website: 'Every physical product has a digital history, allowing you to trace and verify its origins, attributes and ownership.'

Asset registration and exchange

Blockchain can facilitate the recording and trading of a wide variety of assets and not, as we said earlier, only financial instruments. In real estate, it could change the way a local government's property registry operates and is secured.

Imagine if New Orleans had had all those years of records already on a Blockchain before Katrina!

But asset registration and exchange can also make liquid those assets that are traditionally not liquid. This could be done by introducing the exchange of virtual tokens embodying those underlying assets. These tokens – often referred to as Coins – can also represent intellectual or physical property.

Example: Diamond Coin – http://dmcoin.net/

Diamond Coin is a digital currency backed by investment-grade diamonds. You have physical diamonds, they get certified and stored, and you receive an amount of equivalent tokens, aka coins. You can now go online and trade these coins for cash, or simply keep them and recoup your diamond at a later point in time.

How about the financial services arena?

This is where most of the efforts are concentrated today, mostly because it's regarded as a highly inefficient industry desperately needing to cut costs and modernize processes and infrastructure. It has a low degree of automation and still has lots of barriers to innovation, including CEOs fighting to hold on to their seats (and salaries).

R3 (see above under private Blockchain) is a good example here.

Here are three other areas of possible application:

- Securities issuance, trading, clearing, settlement

Blockchain is expected to empower faster settlement, lowering fraud and manipulation risks and simultaneously cutting costs.

Take a look here: https://t0.com/

This proprietary solution belongs to the retail giant Overstock. It's a Blockchain-based private and public equities trading platform which will also enable stock issuing.

- Cash reserves, transfer, collateral management

Thanks to Blockchain, financial institutions could be required to hold a lower amount of cash to cope with cash transfers and settlement requirements: less cash in reserves means lower costs but also speed in execution. This is particularly relevant for international transactions, which currently take days to complete.

Imagine being able to move 50 US dollars from New York to London in seconds!

- Compliance and regulatory affairs

If any transaction is transparently tracked and verified and cannot be altered, it will become easier to identify illegal activities such as fraud, embezzlement, money laundering, etc.

Media

Copyright infringements, anyone? Protecting digital content? Allowing micropayments for using a few seconds of a song, or of a video in YouTube, thus making sure artists get correctly compensated?

Governmental stuff

A voting system on a Blockchain? Unmatched electoral transparency? Accountability for the decisions of the politicians who represent us? More and more countries are already experimenting with e-voting systems, some of them on a Blockchain.

Here is an example: https://followmyvote.com

Internet of Things (IOT) and Machine to Machine (M2M) communication

Now this sounds futuristic but it is not in fact that futuristic…

The Internet of Things (IOT): Every single thing is connected to the Internet.

Thanks to IOT, we can now do cool things like regulating the temperature in our fridge, remotely, using our smartphones.

But what if we outsourced that controlling task to a specialized machine? What if that machine interacted not only with our fridge but also with our smartphone to autonomously arrange any corrective actions needed (e.g. repairs). This would be an example of what the experts call a Machine to Machine (M2M) transaction.

Actually, it's not hard to imagine that these M2M transactions would then also require a form of compensation, meaning 'paying themselves' for services.

How could they do this?

Here an example: https://www.iotatoken.com/

Healthcare

Lots of sensitive information is associated with health: identities, diseases, treatments, payments, etc.

Our health is probably the most private property we have yet, more and more often, data breaches result in private information being made public online.

Imagine if that happened to Estonia, which is among the few digital societies if not the only one at present to have 100% of its medical records online.

What if a Blockchain could manage the entire lifecycle of our medical records? Imagine if we were able to record and store our genomic data on a Blockchain so that it could be used to support scientific investigations.

Some of the above applications are still in development at the time of writing and may undoubtedly appear as visionary: we already know that only a few may turn into successful startups while others will fail completely or simply be forced to change their mission and explore other fronts.

This is perfectly normal when new technology appears but experimenting is key to progress. Since the arrival of the Internet, almost every sector of our society has been on the quest for a better way to cope with new needs such as higher efficiency, more transparency, or simply accessibility where openness is coupled with privacy.

I'm pretty sure some of the answers to these questions can be found around the future development of Blockchain technology since the spectrum of potential applications is infinite.

Chapter Seven: Conclusion

Blockchains are not yet integrated into our daily lives.

Part of the explanation is that the user experience of Blockchain-based applications has so far been poor: it still looks geeky, complex, and unfriendly.
Even the basic terminology results in confusion from time to time.

So, yes: the technology is still pretty much in its infancy but the general consensus seems to be that we're not too far away from that Eureka moment when the technology will mature and become mainstream.

Remember how the Internet used to live behind closed doors, before email, Facebook, Twitter, online banking, and Internet Explorer became popular?

With Blockchains, we're still in that behind-closed-doors phase. Yet at the same time we're less and less detached from the real word. Take Bitcoin as an example. When the UK voted to leave the EU (i.e. Brexit) in 2016, the value of Bitcoin rose by 20%. A similar effect – a rise of almost 20% in the value of Bitcoin – occurred in the same year when the People's Bank of China decided to devalue the renminbi.

Now take a look at this: At the time of writing, Bitcoin's market capitalization is almost 1 billion US dollars. Not bad for just a cryptocurrency that is not even a company selling products like IBM or McDonald's!

Whether we want it or not, we're on the brink of something major. Nobody can yet tell where this is going: The threshold between what we can already see in terms of applications and what we cannot even imagine at this point is definitely blurred!

But rest assured: Blockchain technology is here to stay and it's not immune from gravitational forces. As usual, the greater the number of people using it, the harder it becomes for others to stay away from or resist it.

Once the right consumer application has entered the market so that we, the normal users, can also feel some real benefits, it will be a big boom, roll fast, and forever change the way we operate!

The author name is Piero Martini

I hope you enjoyed this book and that it helped you get a better understanding of what Blockchain technology is about.

If you liked this reading, found it useful or otherwise educative, then I'd really appreciate it if you would post a short review on Amazon.
I do read all the reviews personally so that I can take any feedback, such as suggestions for improvements or other topics you'd like to see addressed in further books, and continue to improve!

Thanks for your support!

Made in the USA
San Bernardino, CA
28 August 2017